A gift for

....

From

....

Date

....

THE
WEEKLY
REST
PROJECT

A CHALLENGE TO JOURNAL, REFLECT, AND RESTORE

◼ ZONDERVAN®

ZONDERVAN

The Weekly Rest Project

Copyright © 2024 by Zondervan

Published in Grand Rapids, Michigan, by Zondervan. Zondervan is a registered trademark of The Zondervan Corporation, L.L.C., a wholly owned subsidiary of HarperCollins Christian Publishing, Inc.

Requests for information should be addressed to customercare@harpercollins.com.

Zondervan titles may be purchased in bulk for educational, business, fundraising, or sales promotional use. For information, please email SpecialMarkets@Zondervan.com.

ISBN 978-0-310-46453-2 (hardcover)

Art direction: Tiffany Forrester
Cover design: Noelle Glaze
Interior Illustrations: Creative Market / Patishop Art, Khrys Art, Lenis
Interior design: Kristy Edwards

Printed in India

24 25 26 27 28 MAI 10 9 8 7 6 5 4 3 2 1

THE
WEEKLY
REST
PROJECT

Contents

Introduction

Rest Is a Gift from God

*On the seventh day—with the canvas of
the cosmos completed—God paused from
His labor and rested. Thus God blessed
day seven and made it special—an* open
time for pause and restoration, a
sacred zone of Sabbath-keeping.

GENESIS 2:2–3 THE VOICE

D o we really think our all-powerful, all-knowing God
needed to rest after just six days of work? Possibly, but
it seems more likely that God *chose* to rest to show us the
importance of resting from our labors. He knew that we would
need an example to follow, and that lesson is just as important
today as it was all those years ago.

Our culture places a lot of emphasis on working hard,
earning your place, and pulling yourself up by your bootstraps,
but a close reading of the Bible reveals a very different
message. God doesn't love you because you work harder than
anyone else. You can't earn your place in heaven through good
works. And God certainly doesn't determine your value by your
use of your bootstraps—quite the opposite.

After all, the Bible isn't full of stories of independent go-
getters who won accolades all on their own by working around
the clock. No, the stories are of people who leaned on God to
achieve great things by saying yes to Him and following His
path, which includes good work, but also always includes rest.

The Sabbath was the first day specifically set aside for something established by God. More holy days and holidays and feasts would come later, but the Sabbath has been with us since creation. It is one of God's first gifts to us, a sacred time to give our bodies and minds a chance to recharge and anchor our weeks in rest and communion with Him. Resting regularly isn't being lazy and doesn't mean that we are shirking our responsibilities. It is simply accepting God's generous gift. Building our lives around weekly rest is the first step in accepting the rhythm of life God laid out for us at the beginning, and it only brings us closer to Him.

Rhythms
of Rest

To everything there is a season, a time
for every purpose under heaven.

ECCLESIASTES 3:1 NKJV

The entire world runs on cycles. Day becomes night. Night becomes day. Winter melts into spring. Spring blooms into summer. Summer fades into autumn. And autumn freezes into winter. Years pass by, and people are born and eventually die, but these cycles that God created remain the same. He set each cycle moving at creation, including the ones that govern our days.

The Bible models this cycle for us. It is a rhythm of work, play, worship, and rest. Days for work, nights for rest, Sabbath each week, and everyone pausing to come together to worship and celebrate for holidays and feasts. Everything in balance to keep us healthy physically, mentally, and spiritually. The seasons have always played a role too. Work was limited by daylight and the weather until very recently. There was less outdoor work to be done in the winter and more time to rest. Now, of course, thanks to technology, we can work anytime and anywhere, even when we shouldn't.

Our modern, busy, go-go-go, I'll-rest-when-I'm-dead mentality doesn't truly disrupt or circumvent the cycle God provided us, even if it feels like working around the clock is some sort of cheat code to getting to the good life. It may lead to financial success, but it always comes at a cost—usually our health and overall well-being. We've turned away from living in community and working together to carry the load in favor of doing it all on our own, in our own ways. As a result, we're a society of people who are sick, unhappy, burned out, lonely, and overwhelmed. And that is definitely not God's plan for us.

Prioritizing rest is about more than catching up on sleep. It's about living our lives in sync with the rhythms God laid out for us that are designed to bring us closer to Him.

The Sabbath Was Made for Man

Then he said to them, "The Sabbath was made for man, not man for the Sabbath."

MARK 2:27 NIV

Keeping the Sabbath has always been an important part of Jewish culture, and as stated in the Ten Commandments, no work was to be done on the Sabbath in order to keep it holy. But in Jesus' time, that had been taken to extremes. It was considered work to put food on the table, to gather water, to do almost anything at all. For many people the Sabbath was not restful; it was stressful.

Jesus was revolutionary in many ways, but at the time, one of the most controversial things He said was, "The Sabbath was made for man, not man for the Sabbath." The Jewish leaders had turned the Sabbath, the day of rest, into a series of rules to be followed. Jesus recognized that for what it was: a perversion of God's original gift of a day of rest. His simple statement said volumes. The Sabbath wasn't some divine test where God was watching for every infraction. It was a generous gift, a sacred day to pause from the hard labor of the week and be refreshed.

What hobbies do you have that refresh you?

....
....
....
....
....

How can you incorporate those into your plans for the Sabbath over the next few weeks?

....
....
....
....
....
....
....
....
....
....
....

WEEK 2

Keep the Sabbath

"Remember the Sabbath day by keeping it holy."

EXODUS 20:8 NIV

God included the Sabbath, a holy day of rest, in His Ten Commandments (Exodus 20:8–10) because of how important it is. There isn't any fluff in the Ten Commandments. There were no superfluous words or extra information, and yet the rule about keeping the Sabbath was the longest one. God wanted it to be very clear that *everyone* was to rest on the Sabbath, not just the wealthiest or most powerful people.

The Sabbath was the most sacred day of the week for God's people in the ancient world. These days, it has become much more difficult to keep a true weekly Sabbath. Weekends get filled with kids' activities, errands, chores, church, and all the tasks that didn't get completed during the busy work week. Many of us also manage to squeeze in answering a few work emails too.

We still, as a society, largely keep the rest of the Ten Commandments, but keeping the Sabbath has fallen by the wayside. It's no less important than it was in Moses' day, and it's time we treated it as such.

Why do you think keeping Sabbath is considered less important now?

....

....

....

....

....

....

How do you generally spend your days off? Do you set aside Sunday (or another day) as a Sabbath?

....

....

....

....

....

....

....

....

....

....

11

A Deeper Sabbath Restores More Fully

*"When you enter the land which I am going to give you, the land will observe a Sabbath to G*OD*. Sow your fields, prune your vineyards, and take in your harvests for six years. But the seventh year the land will take a Sabbath of complete and total rest."*

LEVITICUS 25:2–4 MSG

This edict from God to let the promised land observe a one-year Sabbath to God was probably confusing to the Israelites. After all, a whole year off from planting crops and tending the land must have felt threatening to their food supply. But God knew something that the Israelites didn't: even the land needs rest. Constant planting and growing uses up all the nutrients in the soil, until eventually crops won't grow or growth will be stunted. A year off from growing allows the soil to be replenished.

If time off for replenishment is necessary for something as basic as soil, we, with our incredibly complex bodies and minds, need the same. Observing a Sabbath each week is crucial, but we need more rest than that. Taking longer stretches of time off is important to help replenish ourselves. Seasons where we work less and rest more can help immensely.

If you could take a sabbatical, what would you do to rest and replenish yourself?

....

....

....

....

....

....

....

How can you incorporate some of those activities into your existing periods of rest, even if for just a weekend or holiday?

....

....

....

....

....

....

Intentional Rest

*"Come with me by yourselves to a quiet place
and get some rest." So they went away by
themselves in a boat to a solitary place.*

MARK 6:31–32 NIV

Jesus had a lot of important work to do here on earth,
arguably the *most important* work in history, but He often
made time to rest, as we read about in the Gospels. Just as
God set an example for us when He took a day to rest during
creation, Jesus set an example for us about resting each day.

After spending time with large groups of people, Jesus
took time alone to regain His energy and often sought out
solitary places. After traveling, Jesus needed time to sit, and
water to quench His thirst. Jesus didn't work around the clock.
He slept at night and took naps during the day. He shared
meals with His apostles. He prioritized time alone to pray.

Jesus was limited by His human body here on
earth, and He felt all the pangs and pains that come
with that, just like we do. Instead of pushing past
His own limits, Jesus very intentionally cared for His
body, mind, and soul regularly, just as we should.

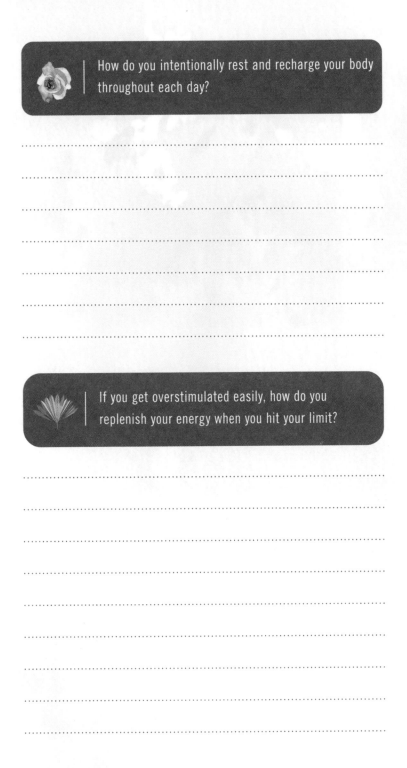

How do you intentionally rest and recharge your body throughout each day?

....
....
....
....
....
....

If you get overstimulated easily, how do you replenish your energy when you hit your limit?

....
....
....
....
....
....
....
....

Praise

Let everything that has breath praise the LORD.

PSALM 150:6 NKJV

Nothing recharges us like time spent with God. Reading Scripture, prayer, and praise are all deeply restorative for our minds and souls. This is why the Sabbath is meant to be a "Sabbath to the Lord." It's not just a day of rest but a day to reconnect with God and thank Him for the blessings of the week. Consistent time spent with God is as important to our overall health as sleep and food.

Many people honor the Sabbath by attending church, but that is certainly not the only way to connect with God each week. Prayer and praise can happen just as easily in the solitude of your home or in the beauty of God's creation as it can in a sanctuary. You can read God's Word as easily alone or with a small, trusted group of believers as you can in an auditorium of thousands.

Communing with God isn't one-size-fits-all. The important thing is to find what works for you and make it a priority.

How does praise and prayer restore you?

....
....
....
....

How do you feel when you go too long without connecting with God in some way?

....
....
....
....
....

How can you be consistent in spending time with God?

....
....
....
....

Feasts and Holy Days

*When it was time, he sat down, all the apostles
with him, and said, "You've no idea how
much I have looked forward to eating this
Passover meal with you before I enter my time
of suffering. It's the last one I'll eat until we
all eat it together in the kingdom of God."*

LUKE 22:14–16 MSG

The Sabbath each week is an important, sacred day for rest and worship, but God also set aside other holidays for celebration, connection, and rest from the usual work and routine. Jesus made sure to stop and celebrate these holy days, feasts, and festivals, including Passover and Hanukkah. One of the first miracles Jesus performed was at a wedding at Cana (John 2:1–12), where He turned water into wine. Jesus knew that times of celebration were important for building connection and community.

Community matters as part of a balanced life. Genuinely connecting with others is how friendships are forged. We all need a network of people to support and encourage us. Time spent resting alone and time spent connecting with others recharge us in different ways, but both are essential.

| What is your favorite holiday to celebrate and why?

....
....
....
....
....

| Do you have a particular tradition that you find especially restorative?

....
....
....
....

| If not, what is one restorative tradition you could add to the holidays?

....
....
....
....

Share in Rest

*Then he said to them, "Go your way. Eat
the fat and drink sweet wine and send
portions to anyone who has nothing
ready, for this day is holy to our Lord."*

NEHEMIAH 8:10

God intended times of rest and the Sabbath to be for *everyone*. But of course, it is easier for some people than others. Money, grief, family estrangement, and other personal issues can all leave time off feeling less than restorative.

The flip side of building a community to support you is being willing to support others as well. Sharing your time and energy with others may sound draining, but there is something profoundly restorative to your heart when you take the time to love others well.

Jesus told us that the most important of God's laws for us are to love Him and to love each other (Matthew 22:36–40). To love others well, we have to get out into our community and connect with one another. Each of us has different skills and a heart for different causes and issues. Find a way to help that speaks to your skills and your heart, and you'll find that helping will restore you in the best possible ways.

How have you helped others in the past? How did this feel restorative?

....

....

....

....

....

....

....

....

How can you plan ahead to help others during the holidays this year?

....

....

....

....

....

....

....

....

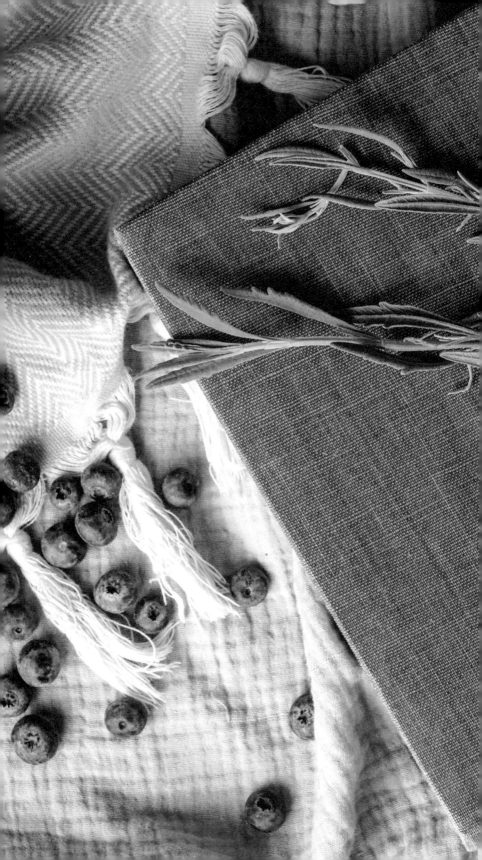

You Aren't Alone

The Lord replied, "My Presence will go
with you, and I will give you rest."

EXODUS 33:14 NIV

When you are struggling, it can be extremely lonely and isolating, even if you do have a top-notch support system of friends and family. The stress and worry can be a constant weight pulling you down and making it difficult to sleep, think clearly, and take steps forward.

Stress sends a message to your body that you are in danger. When we're stressed, our adrenal glands flood our systems with cortisol, a steroid hormone, which gives us increased physical strength and stamina but can also increase anxiety. This is super helpful if you need to outrun a lion, like our ancestors had to do, but not helpful when you need to get a peaceful night's sleep.

Luckily, asking God for help through prayer and connecting with Him through worship can give you back that elusive peace and help you find the rest you need. God will never leave you alone. He will always be there to give you rest, and He will never let you face your battles on your own—if you only ask Him to help.

| How does stress affect your body and your peace?

....
....
....
....

| What do you find most helpful for relieving stress?
  How do prayer and worship factor in?

....
....
....
....
....

| Ask God to help you rest.

....
....
....
....
....

Seek Out God to Be Restored

*Jesus often withdrew to lonely
places and prayed.*

LUKE 5:16 NIV

Jesus is well-known for His sermons and miracles that drew crowds. But Jesus also spent a lot of time between those events alone. He sought out time to abide with God in places where He would not be disturbed.

Close your eyes and imagine the optimal place and way to rest. Are you somewhere serene and dark? Or somewhere light and bright? Are you sleeping or praying or reading or listening to music? What one person finds restful can be something another person finds stressful. We're all different. But one thing is certain: to achieve our best rest, we have to seek it out.

If you need quiet time each evening to process the day and decrease stress, create a quiet corner with a comfortable chair, a cozy blanket, and your Bible and journal. Set an alarm to remind you to take that time each evening or to remind you to turn out the lights and go to sleep.

If you aren't already in the habit of resting well and regularly, it will take some effort to get into the groove, but it will be effort well spent.

| Describe your ideal rest scenario.

....

....

....

....

....

....

....

....

| What is a restful space that you need to create or optimize for yourself?

....

....

....

....

....

....

....

....

....

The Peace of God's Creation

*Then, after the crowd had gone, Jesus went up
to a mountaintop alone (as He had intended
from the start). As evening descended, He
stood alone on the mountain, praying.*

MATTHEW 14:23 The Voice

While it's true that you can find God's peace anywhere, there is something especially effective about seeking God out in the beauty of His creation. From the peaceful rhythm of waves lapping the shore on the beach to the awe-inspiring views from the tops of hills and mountains to the wildflowers blooming on a local hiking trail, God's fingerprints are everywhere in nature.

If you are struggling to get into a restful routine, go outside. Sit with the sun on your face. Lie in a hammock in your backyard and read a good book. Walk around the block while you pray. Go for an overnight camping (or glamping, if that's more your style) trip and look up at the stars. We were created to live in harmony with nature, not to be constantly set apart from it. Seeking out nature will help you get back into sync with the daily and yearly rhythms created by God.

What is your favorite outdoor activity? Is it restful?

....
....
....
....
....
....
....
....

Do you have a favorite place to visit in nature? What makes it your favorite?

....
....
....
....
....
....
....

Pace Yourself

*Let's not allow ourselves to get fatigued
doing good. At the right time we will harvest
a good crop if we don't give up, or quit.*

GALATIANS 6:9 MSG

Have you ever felt like rest was a waste of precious time? Like there was more to do than time to do it in, and rest just wasn't a priority in the moment? Did that feeling last just through whatever crisis you were in, or has it persisted?

You certainly aren't alone if you answered yes to any of those questions. There are times when there is less time to rest, like when you need to work a little overtime to pay for an emergency car repair. The problem is that once you fall into the trap of not resting, it's very difficult to get back out, and you can face burnout.

The only way to avoid burnout is to pace yourself. The world needs you whole and healthy, and that means you have to rest and take care of yourself.

| How have you fallen into the trap of not resting?

....

....

....

....

....

....

....

| What is going on in your life that is making you feel burned out?

....

....

....

....

....

....

....

....

Tender Care

*I called on the L*ORD *in distress; the L*ORD
answered me and set me in a broad place.

PSALM 118:5 NKJV

S ometime between childhood and the beginning of
adulthood, many of us become convinced that we have to
do everything ourselves. That asking for help or letting others
care for us is shameful in some way, that it makes us weak or
pathetic or less than. But that really couldn't be further from
the truth. There is no passage in Scripture that says anything
of the sort.

What God does say, over and over, is that He wants us to
call on Him. That He will provide for us. That He loves us and
wants to care for us. It's one thing to read that,
but it's quite another to truly *believe* it—to believe
it so completely that we let those words change
the way we move through the world. After all, we are
deserving of rest, and it's important to ask for the
help we need from God. To let Him and others care for
us. To accept that we don't have to earn God's love.

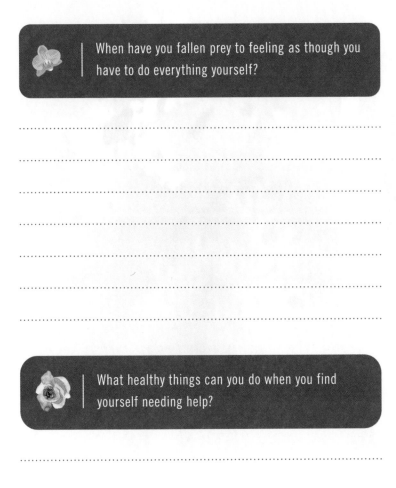

When have you fallen prey to feeling as though you have to do everything yourself?

....
....
....
....
....
....
....

What healthy things can you do when you find yourself needing help?

....
....
....
....
....
....
....
....
....

Let the Seasons Lead You

*"While the earth remains, seedtime and
harvest, cold and heat, summer and
winter, day and night, shall not cease."*

GENESIS 8:22

Nothing in nature blooms all year long. And neither can you. Just like you would never expect to see roses opening up in a blizzard, you can't expect yourself to be at your absolute best and brightest year-round.

The seasons are a cycle designed to balance rest and work, replenishment and growth. The rain and warmer weather of spring coax new life to grow. In the summer, plants bloom into maturity. The cooler air and shorter days of autumn begin nature's season of rest. In winter the old plants decay to become nutrients and fertilizer for the new growth of spring.

Everyone loves the new life of spring and the blooms of summer, but those things could not happen without the rest and replenishment afforded in autumn and winter. It is in those stages of rest when plants collect nutrients and deep, strong roots are able to grow. We need the same chances to rest and replenish so we are able to grow and bloom to our fullest.

Do you have seasons when you are able to rest more deeply? What does that look like for you?

....

....

....

....

....

....

How do you operate without deep roots grown during times of rest?

....

....

....

....

....

....

....

....

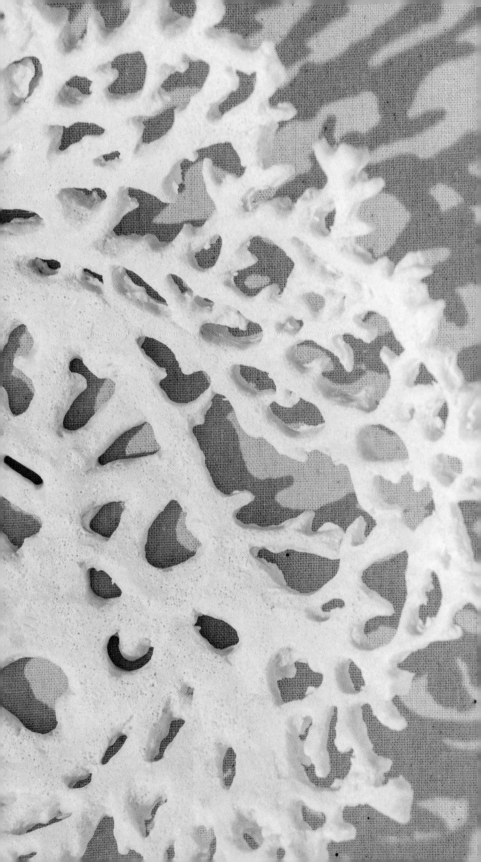

Physical Rest

Your mind *will be* clear, *free from*
fear; when you lie down to rest, *you*
will be refreshed by *sweet sleep.*

PROVERBS 3:24 THE VOICE

hen we think of rest, we most often think of physical rest. That is the easiest place to start incorporating better rest habits into our routines, but it is about more than just sleep. Another way to say rest is *self-care*. The building blocks of self-care are nutrition, exercise, play, and, of course, sleep. Eating nutritious food and drinking plenty of water make it easier for our bodies to do all the things they need to do, including rest. Exercise helps tire us out physically, and we naturally want to rest afterward. Play helps us relax in ways that other things can't. And of course, sleep is self-explanatory, even if most of us aren't getting enough of it.

How is your physical rest? Are you seeking out sweet sleep by taking care of yourself well, or are you putting your body last in your priorities? Move self-care up the list, and as you are kind and gentle with your body, rest will come more easily.

Your Body Is a Temple

*Do you not know that your body is a
temple of the Holy Spirit within you?*

1 CORINTHIANS 6:19 NASB

This verse is often used to shame people's choices. Think, "Why are you eating that cheeseburger? Don't you know your body is a temple?" But what if, instead of feeling shame when we read this, we let it make us feel proud?

Our bodies are strong and beautifully crafted to fulfill God's purpose. They are precious and wonderfully made. They are worth caring for, no matter their shape, size, or abilities. And these temples deserve to be treated kindly and reverently.

Everybody is different. What your body needs won't be exactly the same as everyone else you know, and that's okay. Some people feel best eating all veggies and running every day. Others prefer more protein and lifting weights. Some people get regular massages while others like to soak away their stress with a daily bath. Listen carefully to your own body and give it what it needs so it is ready to go and do the things you want to do.

In what ways are you treating your body like a temple?

....
....
....
....
....
....
....

What does your self-care routine look like when you feel great?

....
....
....
....
....
....
....
....
....

Rest from Illness

The LORD *sustains them on their sickbed and*
restores them from their bed of illness.

PSALM 41:3 NIV

Rest is especially important when you get sick. Even something as mild as a cold can become much worse if you don't take the time to rest and let your body heal.

Getting sick is never going to be convenient. It's not like you can plan ahead for it or push it off to a less busy time. Rescheduling meetings and appointments isn't easy, but it is important to take the time you need to recover and trust that things won't fall apart without you there.

We all get sick sometimes. It is not actually a show of strength to keep going despite how awful you feel. It just shows that you put yourself last. The real show of strength is to acknowledge that your health is important and that your body deserves to be cared for. It's a responsible and healthy move to take the time to rest so you can give your best when you have recovered.

If you have ever gone to work or school still ill, why did you feel like you couldn't take time off?

....
....
....
....

Were you able to accomplish your usual level of work? Or did you drag through the day barely getting anything done?

....
....
....
....
....

What might have happened if you had just waited to recover and come back feeling well?

....
....
....

The Gift of Sleep

He grants sleep to those he loves.

PSALM 127:2 NIV

If you've ever had trouble falling or staying asleep, you know that sleep is a gift that shouldn't be taken for granted. But when there doesn't feel like enough time in the day, so many of us are guilty of staying up too late to finish work or just to have a little time alone at the end of a demanding day. We get sucked into watching TV or mindlessly scrolling through social media.

We *know* that these things aren't restful, but we do them anyway because our mental loads are too heavy. We can really be our own worst enemies.

To sleep well, most experts suggest avoiding blue light from digital devices for a half hour before sleep, setting a time for lights out and sticking with it, avoiding caffeine in the afternoon and evening, and making sure your sleep space is dark, cool, and comfortable. But everyone is different. You may want to add a sound machine, use lavender room spray or essential oils, or take a warm bath every evening before bed—whatever helps you relax and prepare your body and mind for rest.

What habits are keeping you from setting a consistent sleep schedule and sticking to it?

What will you include in your bedtime routine?

45

Through the Storm

*Then Jesus got into the boat and started across
the lake with his disciples. Suddenly, a fierce
storm struck the lake, with waves breaking
into the boat. But Jesus was sleeping.*

MATTHEW 8:23–24 NLT

Rest can be a revolutionary act of faith. Choosing to rest
as laid out by God, even in the midst of the storms of life,
shows a deep and abiding level of trust in His protection. It's
easy to make healthy choices, fall asleep at night, and find time
to relax when life is easy. It is much more difficult to do when
it feels like life keeps handing you one disaster after another,
your health is poor, or you are struggling to get the things you
need just to stay afloat.

Faith is much the same. It's easy to trust
in God's provision when things are good, but
much, much harder when everything feels like
it's falling apart.

Tonight, choose faith. Lie down in bed and
choose to rest. Give your worries and struggles
over to God and trust that He has it under
control. Then let your faith in Him lull you to sleep.

How can you choose rest as an act of faith?

....
....
....
....
....
....
....

What holds you back from letting God handle your worries?

....
....
....
....
....
....
....
....

Ask for Help

*Bear one another's burdens, and
so fulfill the law of Christ.*

GALATIANS 6:2

Finding time for rest when your schedule is packed to the brim can be tough. When you are juggling work commitments, friendships, family time or parenting, and volunteer commitments, plus trying to manage all the everyday tasks like laundry and grocery shopping, how do you squeeze in more rest? You ask for help.

Call on your community. Ask God to send helpers your way. Trust Him to work in big ways, and then start asking around for the smaller things you need. Ask your mom to come help you clean your place or your friends to take your volunteer slots. Ask your partner to take on more parenting duties and your kids to step up around the house.

Don't feel guilty asking for help. If any of *your* people asked you for help, you'd be there in a heartbeat. Let them do the same for you, even if it's a little uncomfortable to ask. It's worth putting yourself out there.

Which items on your to-do list could be delegated? Who could you ask to help?

....
....
....
....
....
....

Ask God to send helpers your way.

....
....
....
....
....
....
....
....
....

Work Hard, Rest Hard

*Come to me, all who labor and are heavy
laden, and I will give you rest.*

MATTHEW 11:28

There's a stigma around rest in our society. The appearance of being busy and putting in extra time usually matters more than the amount of work actually accomplished. Our culture says that only lazy people take time off, while hard workers put in extra hours. But plenty of hard workers get their work done *and* take time to rest. That balance is the goal.

To achieve that balance, you'll have to start saying yes to rest, which means you'll have to say no to other things—even work! When you put in a full day of work, you absolutely deserve a full night of rest. It is okay to say no to those extra hours, especially when you have accomplished everything you are supposed to. It doesn't make you lazy. And if you do need to put in some overtime, you need to match it with some extra rest.

Realigning your expectations about what a good day of work truly looks like will be instrumental in figuring out what a more balanced life looks like for *you*. And once you can picture that balanced life, it will be so much easier to achieve it.

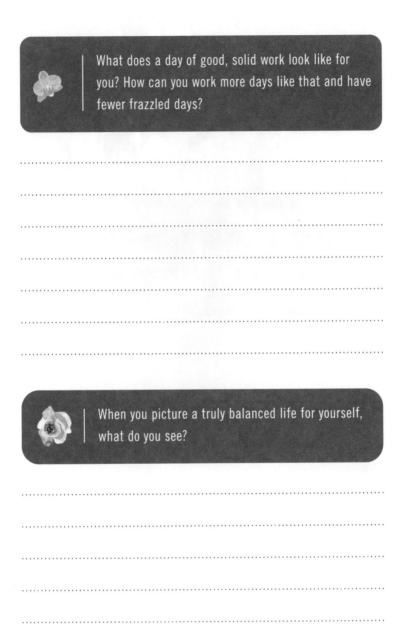

What does a day of good, solid work look like for you? How can you work more days like that and have fewer frazzled days?

....

....

....

....

....

....

When you picture a truly balanced life for yourself, what do you see?

....

....

....

....

....

....

....

Listen to Your Body

*Jesus, tired as he was from the
journey, sat down by the well.*

JOHN 4:6 NIV

Eight hours of sleep each night is the current recommended guideline for adults, but that may not be enough rest for you. God created each of us uniquely, and our bodies have unique needs. Eight hours may be plenty for someone in her early twenties but not nearly enough for someone in her forties. The same is true for exercise recommendations and the amount of water and calories you need each day.

Guidelines can be helpful for getting started with a more restful schedule, but ultimately you know your body best. It's time to tune out all that noise and focus on what actually works for you. Even Jesus sat down to rest when He needed it. You can too.

Take time throughout each day for quick body check-ins. How are your energy, hunger, and thirst levels? Do you need to take a break for a quick walk outside or maybe just rest your eyes for ten minutes? The more you take time to pay attention to your body, the more clearly you will be able to actually identify what you need.

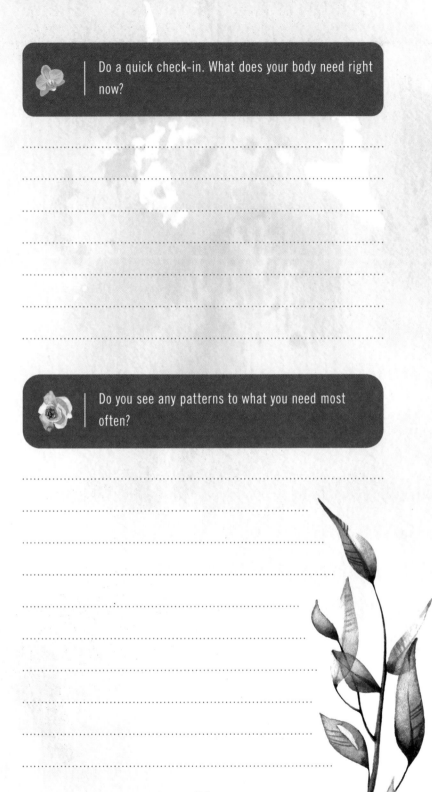

Do a quick check-in. What does your body need right now?

....

....

....

....

....

....

Do you see any patterns to what you need most often?

....

....

....

....

....

....

....

....

....

....

Play Time

*He will yet fill your mouth with laughter,
and your lips with shouting.*

JOB 8:21

You would technically be getting plenty of rest if you worked all day, came home, ate dinner, and then went to bed, but you wouldn't actually be living a balanced, restful life. Play and fun are important parts of rest that often get overlooked. We all need joy in our lives. Joy literally makes our brains happier and healthier and helps us relax.

Playing and having fun increase your body's production of feel-good neurotransmitters such as oxytocin, serotonin, and dopamine, improving brain activity and decreasing stress. Your brain has over 100 million nerve cells, and they are activated when you do things that bring you joy. This can include hobbies like creating art, cycling, or gardening as well as more childlike play such as jumping on a trampoline or building a fort with your kids.

If you have good sleep habits but your life has been anything but restful, it may be that you need to incorporate more fun and joy into your days.

When was the last time you did something just for fun?

....
....
....
....
....

What hobbies bring you joy?

....
....
....
....

What fun or joyful things could you do this week?

....
....
....
....
....

Daily Bread

Give us today our daily bread.

MATTHEW 6:11 NIV

Living a more restful, balanced life includes being thoughtful and intentional about what you put into your body. The food and drinks you consume have almost as much of an effect on your energy levels as your sleep schedule does. Drinking plenty of water and eating whole, nutritious food really can help you feel your best.

A lot of diets are out there, but unless your doctor has you on a specific diet, it's worth taking the time to figure out which foods work well for you and which don't, instead of blindly following someone else's plan. Eat more of what makes your body feel good and less of what doesn't. Be mindful of how you feel after eating, and keep adding to your list of great foods for you. Over time, you'll create a customized diet that helps you feel your best.

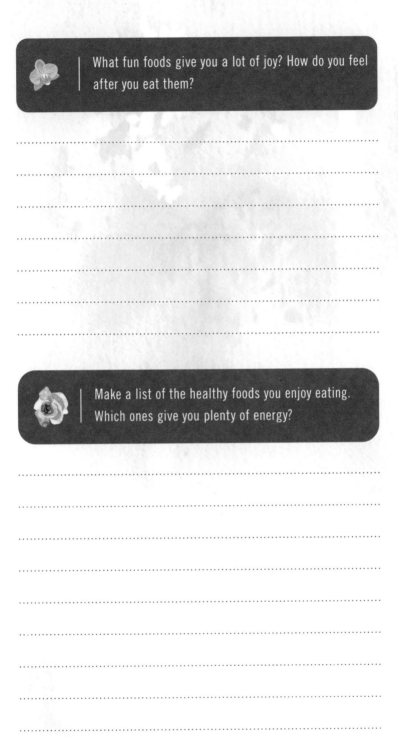

What fun foods give you a lot of joy? How do you feel after you eat them?

....
....
....
....
....
....

Make a list of the healthy foods you enjoy eating. Which ones give you plenty of energy?

....
....
....
....
....
....
....
....
....

Repent to Find Rest

When I refused to admit my wrongs, I was
miserable. . . . When I finally saw my own
lies, *I owned up to my sins before You.* . . . *You*
lifted and *carried away the guilt of my sin.*

PSALM 32:3, 5 The Voice

Guilt and shame are enemies of rest. When you know you
have done something wrong or hurt someone, it can
really weigh down your thoughts and mood, keeping you up
at night and making you feel awful physically and mentally.
Luckily, repentance is the fix for that.

The idea of repenting may not feel restful (probably the
opposite!), but it is truly the only way to get out from under the
shame and guilt. Start with prayer and ask forgiveness from
God. Let His grace lift that weight from your shoulders.

Then, if you have hurt someone else, apologize to them
as well and see if you can make things right. They may not be
ready to forgive you, and while that won't feel great, that's not
really the point. You can't force someone to let go of their hurt
feelings or to trust you again if you have betrayed that trust.

Repentance doesn't hinge on anyone accepting your
apology. It is about what's happening in *your* heart, not anyone
else's. When you have repented and
forgiven yourself, you can let the past go
and move forward with a lesson learned and a
clearer conscience.

| What do you need to repent for right now?

....
....
....
....
....

| Pray and ask God for forgiveness. How do you feel?

....
....
....
....
....

| What can you do to make it right with others? With
yourself?

....
....
....
....

Trust in God's Protection

I lie down and sleep. I wake up again,
because the Lord takes care of me.

PSALM 3:5 NIrV

God is taking care of you all the time, both in ways you can sense and ways you can't. When life gets complicated or difficult, it doesn't mean that God has stopped protecting you. It just might mean that you can't perceive or understand that protection. He has the full, big picture, while you can see only a small portion.

Stressful and difficult things will happen—that's a guarantee—but that doesn't mean that God isn't working for your good behind the scenes. There is no way for us to know how our losses, illnesses, and struggles are being used by Him. Stressing and trying to control everything ourselves won't get us anywhere, and it usually ends up costing us rest. We have to have faith in God's control, even when the plan seems to make no sense.

Every day that we get to wake up and keep living is a gift. Hold tight to God's promised protection and rest easy, knowing that He takes care of you, both when you can see it and when you can't.

What in your life are you trying to control with an iron grip?

....
....
....
....

Is it costing you rest? How can you let go of that in faith?

....
....
....
....

Have you had times when something made no sense but actually turned out to be for your best? How do you think God was working there?

....
....
....
....

Ask for Strength

*They who wait for the LORD shall renew
their strength; they shall mount up with
wings like eagles; they shall run and not
be weary; they shall walk and not faint.*

ISAIAH 40:31

We all get tired. From midday sleepiness all the way up to bone-weary, deeply exhausted, on-the-brink-of-insanity tired.

There will be times in life where you feel like it's impossible to get up each morning and keep going. You will grieve with your entire body and soul when you lose someone dear to you. You will get sick and feel pain. You will lie awake in bed at night wracked by guilt or shame or anxiety, unable to find the rest you need. None of us come out of life unscathed by these things.

When you find yourself there, please remember that you are not alone and that you can ask for help. God is right there with you, and there is nothing He cannot do. No situation He cannot fix. You might not always understand His help or why things play out the way that they do, but you can count on His promise to help when you need it.

Describe a time you felt so exhausted that you couldn't make it through another day.

....
....
....
....
....
....
....
....

What did you do when you felt that way? How did you keep going?

....
....
....
....
....
....
....
....

Eternal Life

The fear of the LORD leads to life,
and whoever has it rests satisfied;
he will not be visited by harm.

PROVERBS 19:23

This life is not the end of your story. It is only the beginning. When you follow Jesus, you know that the ultimate rest awaits you after this life is over.

We see that promise over and over again in the Bible, so we know it's true, but there is a difference between knowing and *knowing*. Until we join God in heaven, it is impossible to understand what it will be like. Our imaginations can never do it justice because we don't have a frame of reference for it.

The truth is that while you deeply feel the stressors and difficulties of this life, they are temporary. They cannot do you permanent harm because you have eternal life in heaven to look forward to. The same is true for the good things. They seem amazing now, but they are nothing compared to the good that awaits you.

When life feels overwhelming and exhausting, remind yourself of the truth that this life is but a mist, here one day and gone the next. Hold God's promise of heaven in your heart and mind, and let it soothe you into rest.

| How do you imagine heaven?

....

....

....

....

....

| What do you most hope to see and feel there?

....

....

....

....

....

| What are you most excited to leave behind on earth?

....

....

....

....

....

Mental Rest

Don't fret or worry. Instead of worrying,
pray. Let petitions and praises shape your
worries into prayers, letting God know your
concerns. Before you know it, a sense of
God's wholeness, everything coming together
for good, will come and settle you down.
It's wonderful what happens when Christ
displaces worry at the center of your life.

PHILIPPIANS 4:6–7 MSG

Physical rest isn't always easy, but at least it is relatively straightforward. Mental rest, on the other hand, is a bit more complicated to pin down. After all, what stresses someone else may not bother you at all. Anxiety could keep you up at night as you worry over things that could go wrong, or you could be kept awake by all the ideas you have and things you want to do. Maybe your inner voice is constantly berating you for the ways you've messed up, or perhaps it compares you to everyone around you, and you feel like you always come up short.

Your challenges and concerns aren't the same as anyone else's, so what helps you calm your thoughts and find peace in your mind will be personal too. Some people turn to meditation or yoga, others pour out their worries to a friend or therapist, and others shove their thoughts and feelings down and hope they will go away if they ignore them long enough. All those methods may help for a little while, but none of them can give your mind true rest.

The only thing we can *all* count on to give us the mental rest we so desperately need is God Himself. He is always there to calm our worries, smooth our racing thoughts, and quiet those inner voices that tell us that we aren't enough and can never measure up.

Whenever you realize that your mind is in turmoil and rest feels incredibly far away, your first step should be to pray. Ask God for His peace. And then lay out everything you are struggling with and ask Him for His help. Let Him carry away your worries and replace them with the serenity that only He can provide.

Worries Keep Rest at Bay

Worrying does not do any good;
who here can claim to add even an
hour to his life by worrying?

MATTHEW 6:27 THE VOICE

We all worry. But worrying doesn't actually get you anywhere. All it does is use up your mental energy, stress you out, and leave you exhausted.

Do you believe that God is in control? If your answer is yes, then what can you hope to accomplish with your worrying that God can't easily handle?

Worrying robs you of rest by keeping you awake and using up precious energy, and it also separates you from God. Trusting that God is in control is an act of faith, but worrying undermines that faith. The unchecked worries running through your brain mean that you still somehow think you can control your circumstances, that it is up to you instead of God to fix whatever needs fixing and to do whatever needs doing. You build up a barrier between you and God, worry by worry, until you are boxed in and alone.

It's time to rest. Give God your worries and let Him give you His peace in return. Let those walls come down.

What have you worried about for a long time that you need to give to God?

....
....
....
....
....
....

Why do you think you keep coming back to this particular worry over and over?

....
....
....
....
....
....
....
....

In Your Own Head

In peace I will lie down and sleep, for you alone, Lord, make me dwell in safety.

PSALM 4:8 NIV

Our minds have an amazing capacity to hold so many memories. So why does it seem like our minds hang on most tightly to the bad, embarrassing, or ridiculous memories? You aren't alone if you find yourself reliving an awkward interaction for weeks.

Our brains are wired to help us learn from our mistakes. If an encounter doesn't go well, our brains decide we need to learn something from it. So that memory gets trotted out over and over in the hopes that we won't ever make the same mistake again. And yes, we can learn a lot from past missteps. But after a certain point, there isn't anything left to learn, and those memories just make us feel small and undermine our confidence. Our ugliest memories eventually become the voices in our heads that can hurt us the most.

All of those negative voices shout loudly, keeping us from rest and trying to drown out God's voice. His is the only voice that speaks complete and total truth and can bring peace to our minds. This week, do your best to quiet your mind and let God's voice be the one you hear.

74

Which is the loudest voice in your head? Is it God? Your best friend cheering you on? The bully from middle school?

....
....
....
....

How does it make you feel? Is it a mostly positive voice or a negative one?

....
....
....
....

What sorts of things does that voice tell you when you are lying in bed trying to sleep at night?

....
....
....
....

Rest from Shame

"In repentance and rest is your salvation,
in quietness and trust is your strength."

ISAIAH 30:15 NIV

There is another name for the cacophony of voices saying negative things in your head. It's shame. It's that painful feeling you get when you think back on something mean or foolish or embarrassing you did.

Sometimes shame is warranted and helpful. If you do something purposefully to hurt someone else, shame can prompt you to apologize and make things right. But more often than not, shame only serves to hurt you and wear you out. You shouldn't still be feeling ashamed about that time in ninth grade when you forgot your speech in front of the class. Time rarely dulls shame, and even perspective doesn't always dispel it because it isn't always rational.

Running through unpleasant moments over and over again in your head not only isn't restful, but it also actively saps you of mental energy and often keeps you up at night. Talk to God about these things you've been carrying for too long. Ask for His help carrying them, but also for healing for your heart.

Are you holding on to shame from your childhood? Why do you think it's still with you?

....

....

....

....

....

....

Have you talked these things over with a therapist? A friend? God? How has that helped?

....

....

....

....

....

....

....

....

....

Rest from Grief

*"Blessed are those who mourn,
for they shall be comforted."*

MATTHEW 5:4 NKJV

G rief is exhausting on every level. It wears you out physically, mentally, and spiritually. And there is no quick fix or ideal way to grieve. It's messy and convoluted, and it certainly doesn't progress in a straight line. Grief feels lonely and overwhelming and painful, and it is isolating.

God knows how debilitating grief is because Jesus experienced it Himself, such as when His friend Lazarus died. He felt loss. He wept. He was angry. He hurt. He felt it as a human, but He also feels it alongside each of us when we mourn.

When we lose someone or something deeply important to us, it can shake our faith. We can't know God's plans or why that loss had to happen. But grief is not the enemy of faith. God can handle our questions and our anger and our hurt. He won't leave us in our grief alone. He will comfort us and share hope in the darkest times because He has already conquered death (John 16:33). Knowing that doesn't mean grief won't hurt, but it does mean that we can ask God for rest and comfort when we're grieving.

| What or who are you grieving for currently?

....
....
....
....
....

| How has that grief affected your rest?

....
....
....
....

| Do you know anyone grieving? How could you come alongside them to help give them rest and relief?

....
....
....
....
....

Lighten Your Load

And he said to his disciples, "Therefore I tell you, do not be anxious about your life."

LUKE 12:22

How many hundreds of tasks, plans, communications, and scheduling issues run through your brain every day? Do you find your mind wandering to other things you need to do even while trying to accomplish simple tasks?

Today we are dealing with a more complicated world than ever existed previously. Technology means we are subjected to mental and physical stimulation from the moment we turn off our phone alarm in the morning until the moment we plug in that same phone to recharge at night. And all of that weighs on us and makes it more difficult to truly rest.

Our world is not becoming simpler or easier to manage. But we do have an option available to us. We can ask God for help. Tell God everything on your mind. Lay out the problems and options and variables, just like you would to your most trusted friend, and ask Him to manage the load. Then wait and watch God work, because He will find ways to give you rest.

| What things are weighing heavy on your mind today?

....

....

....

....

....

....

| What part of your load do you need to give to God?

....

....

....

....

....

....

....

....

....

Selah

*Be angry, but sin not; commune with your own
hearts on your beds, and be silent.* Selah

PSALM 4:4 RSV

Have you ever heard the expression "Don't go to bed angry"? The sentiment of not letting a fight or anger fester for too long is good, as that can lead to bitterness, but that doesn't mean it is always the best option. Sometimes you need a break to process your feelings before you are ready to let go of anger.

It is interesting that Psalm 4:4 ends with *selah*, a word that has long puzzled biblical scholars. Their best guess is that *selah* indicated a pause or a musical rest. A moment to catch your breath if you are singing or to let the previous notes die away if playing an instrument. When you are overwhelmed by anger or other strong emotions, as indicated in this verse, you need a rest to process those big feelings so that they don't lead you to make choices you will regret later. You literally need a *selah*, a rest, a pause to let your emotions settle and take a breath before you continue.

This week, try to incorporate *selah* into each day, whenever you have strong feelings, and see how it feels.

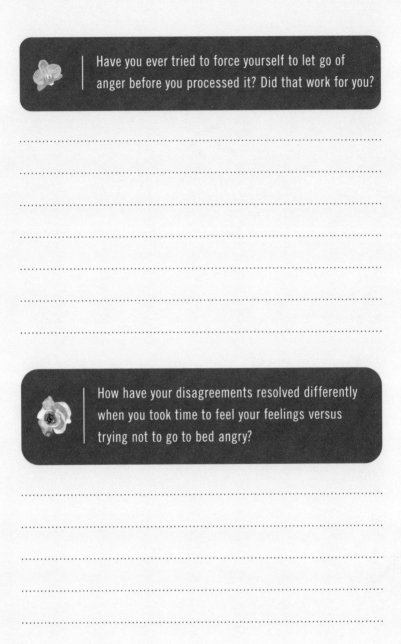

Have you ever tried to force yourself to let go of anger before you processed it? Did that work for you?

....
....
....
....
....
....
....

How have your disagreements resolved differently when you took time to feel your feelings versus trying not to go to bed angry?

....
....
....
....
....
....
....

Put Your Burdens Down

*Since God cares for you, let Him carry
all your burdens and worries.*

1 PETER 5:7 THE VOICE

You make hundreds of decisions each day, from the trivial ones (like what to wear or whether to make a cup of coffee) to the important ones (like how to manage your money or who to befriend). All of those decisions require mental energy, and eventually that adds up.

Have you ever gotten to the end of the day and felt completely unable to decide what you wanted for dinner? That's decision fatigue. Or have you been excited for a day off but then felt too tired to pick a fun activity, so you just ended up lying around? The busier and more complicated your life, the worse it gets.

When you use up all your mental bandwidth on small, inconsequential decisions, you have less patience and energy to make the big, important decisions. As a result, those big decisions feel even more burdensome than they really are, even the good kind of big decisions. And all of that robs you of your mental peace.

This week, pay attention to all the decisions you make. In what ways are you experiencing decision fatigue?

....

....

....

....

Which decisions could you cut out by planning ahead, like choosing your outfits for the week on Sunday evening?

....

....

....

....

What are some big decisions you have struggled with lately?

....

....

....

Rest for the Soul

Truly my soul finds rest in God; my salvation comes from him.

PSALM 62:1 NIV

Have you ever felt soul tired? It's the feeling you get when you watch yet another senseless tragedy on the news or when an injustice makes your heart break. We live here on an imperfect earth for now. But soul weariness happens when we look around and are reminded that *this* is not our home.

God's kingdom isn't filled with violence, injustice, and hate. There, we won't ever feel like we can't possibly win, despite our best efforts, because God has already won. There, loss and hate and grief won't be able to touch us because God will already have His arms around us.

Sometimes it's cold comfort to know that there is somewhere better waiting when it's all so real and visceral here on earth. But that little flame of hope can be nurtured. We aren't in control, and we may not win the battle today, but we can still wade in there and help with God on our side. Helping to make earth a little more like God's kingdom with our words, actions, kindness, and care will give our souls rest enough to see us through.

What things make your soul weary?

....

....

....

....

....

In what ways can you contribute to helping others?

....

....

....

....

....

If you can't help directly, is there a way you can help indirectly?

....

....

....

....

The Sleep of the Righteous

The righteous person is taken away from evil,
he enters into peace; they rest in their beds,
each one who walked in his upright way.

ISAIAH 57:1–2 NASB

Do you consistently choose to do what is right? When we choose to follow Christ, His forgiveness becomes ours. But that doesn't mean that we can do whatever we want, and so it's okay because we are already forgiven. As Christians, we are held to a higher standard because we have a guide for how we should live and act. Jesus didn't have to interpret God's meaning. He lived out God's rules perfectly. He is the template.

If you are struggling to find rest, look at your actions lately. If you are living out of alignment with your values and acting in ways that you know are wrong, it will eventually take a toll on you. Living in the rhythm God laid out for us also means living His way. When you let God change your life and heart and soul to align with His, rest will find you easily.

What might you be doing or thinking this week that is not right?

....
....
....
....

How can you shift your actions to be more in alignment with Christ?

....
....
....
....

Ask God to change your heart so that your values are one with His.

....
....
....
....

Perfect Peace

*You keep him in perfect peace whose mind
is stayed on you, because he trusts in you.*

ISAIAH 26:3

Some of the biggest barriers to mental peace and health
are the lies we tell ourselves, such as "You haven't done
enough," "You don't have enough," and "You aren't loveable."
Lies like that can be really convincing. They make you feel like
you can't win.

If you are what you do, how can you ever do enough?

If you are what you have, how can you ever have enough?

If you don't deserve love, how can you ever earn it?

If your worth is determined by others, how can you ever
stop trying to please them?

Those lies can easily trick you into believing them until
you hold them up against God's truth:

God says you are made in His image.

God says you are valuable.

God says you are loved.

God says you are His.

Regardless of what you've done or haven't done or what's
been done to you, God loves you just as you are right now. If you
are who God says you are, you don't need to do or acquire or
please anyone. You can rest in His peace and His truth.

What are some of the more convincing lies you tell yourself?

....
....
....
....
....
....
....

This week, spend time in Scripture and write down verses that help you see who God says you are.

....
....
....
....
....
....
....
....

Anxiety to Joy

*When my anxious thoughts multiply within
me, Your comfort delights my soul.*

PSALM 94:19 NASB

The Bible is full of suffering: Job, Elijah, Hagar, Jeremiah, Hannah, Solomon, and Ruth (just to name a few). Over a third of the Psalms are psalms of lament. There is an entire book called Lamentations. If the Bible doesn't hide these stories of struggle and suffering, then why do we think we have to hide ours?

Many of us don't talk about our pain because we don't want to be a burden to others. Or maybe we believe others will think that our faith is lacking or that we've done something wrong and brought the pain on ourselves. But it seems clear that God would much rather we cry out in pain to Him than walk away from Him. God can handle our sorrow.

Jesus meets us where we are, not where we pretend to be.

The most common command in the Bible is this: "Fear not." But God usually doesn't leave it at that. He follows it often with, "for I am with you." God always gives us His presence. And His presence is rest and peace and joy when we need it most.

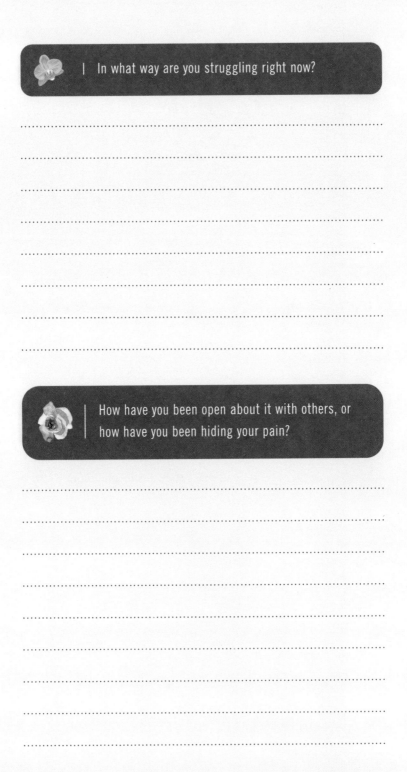

| In what way are you struggling right now?

....

....

....

....

....

....

....

How have you been open about it with others, or
how have you been hiding your pain?

....

....

....

....

....

....

....

....

....

Replenished

*"For I will satisfy the weary soul, and
every languishing soul I will replenish."*

JEREMIAH 31:25

J esus often withdrew to be alone and pray. It seems safe
to assume that all the preaching, healing, and teaching
Jesus did depleted Him physically, mentally, and emotionally.
Spending time in a quiet place abiding in God in prayer
replenished Him and helped Him keep going. If Jesus needed
to withdraw often to be replenished, shouldn't we?

The world is distracting and overstimulating. Everyday life
wears us out. There is no way to truly replenish our reserves
without stepping away from the chaos so that we can rest.
And when we face struggles and challenges, we get depleted
that much faster. The busier and higher-profile Jesus and His
ministry became, the more often He withdrew to rest with His
Father.

We often can't hear ourselves think, let alone hear God
speak to us amid all the noise. How can we let Him guide our
lives if we can't hear Him? We need silence and space and time
to listen to God. If we want God to replenish us, we have to
make space for Him.

> How can you create more space on your calendar to actually rest and be replenished by God?

....
....
....
....
....
....
....

> Where and when do you find yourself able to rest in silence and let God in?

....
....
....
....
....
....
....
....
....

Be Still

"Be still, and know that I am God."

PSALM 46:10

The world is so noisy and complicated. Even if we choose to live more simply, it's impossible to get past how many things we need to think about, figure out, plan for, accomplish, and do. Whether we are asleep or awake, our minds are constantly working, so of course they get tired.

Luckily, there is one constant, one truth that we can focus on completely to find peace and rest, and that's God. When you feel overwrought, overstimulated, or overemotional, lean into the truth that God is so much bigger than this world and everything in it. He's bigger than your problems and worries and hang-ups. He's bigger than your successes and disappointments and all the moments in between.

This week, take time at the beginning and end of each day to be still and focus solely on knowing and trusting God, on connecting to Him, and on letting Him fill you with His perfect peace and rest.

Try being still now and just resting in God's presence. Ask for His help to focus.

....

....

....

....

....

| How did you feel before doing that?

....

....

....

....

| How do you feel afterward?

....

....

....

....

....

Intentional
Rest

There still remains a place of rest, a true
Sabbath, for the people of God because those
who enter into salvation's rest lay down their
labors in the same way that God entered
into a Sabbath rest from His. So let us move
forward to enter this rest, so that none of us
fall into the kind of faithless disobedience
that prevented them from entering.

HEBREWS 4:9–11 THE VOICE

This is *your* life. Your one chance to walk this earth and make a difference. To experience all the world has to offer. And it is entirely up to you what you do with that life. You are the only person who gets to decide how you spend your days and nights. You are the only person who gets to decide where you go and who you spend your time with and what you do. You get to choose the rhythm of your life. You can lean into a constantly busy schedule, or you can turn to face God and follow the gentler rhythm He laid out from the beginning.

If you've been sprinting for years, barely pausing to rest, and making decision after decision that requires you to continue that pace, you won't be able to slow down without causing an uproar somewhere. There will be people who try to convince you to get your running shoes back on and pick up the pace. It will take time to make those changes and convince everyone that you aren't speeding up again. And you will have to keep choosing it over and over until it becomes habit. But it is possible.

Think of everything you've missed in your attempts not to miss anything.

You've missed true, restoring rest. You've missed deep, connective conversations and experiences with the people who matter most to you. You've missed knowing yourself more intimately because moving so quickly doesn't allow for the time to truly experience your emotions. You've missed out on the healing power of relying on God to set and keep the pace for you.

The fast life seems like the right path if you want to succeed, but life has never been a mad dash to the finish line. The whole point is the journey, seeing and experiencing and learning and growing and blooming along the way. Are you ready to slow down and take that journey?

Choose What Is Better

"Martha, Martha," the Lord answered,
"you are worried and upset about many
things . . . Mary has chosen what is better,
and it will not be taken away from her."

LUKE 10:41–42 NIV

Martha was busy preparing a meal for Jesus and others, while her sister Mary sat at Jesus' feet. Poor Martha gets a bad rap as the sister who wouldn't slow down and be present with Jesus. But Martha was serving everyone in her home, which was something Jesus preached often. She wasn't wrong to be offering hospitality. And it really doesn't feel like Jesus was scolding her. Instead, it feels like He was trying to take the burden of being busy off her shoulders. He was inviting her in, calling her to rest in His presence. Yet she was so distracted by her activities that she was missing out on that intimacy with Him.

God is always with us. But if we are so busy and focused on the mundane, we can miss Him. Do you really want to be so busy hustling that you don't see all that He is inviting you in to during that time?

Rest allows us to slow down and be fully present with our Lord.

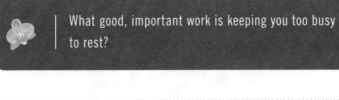

What good, important work is keeping you too busy to rest?

....
....
....
....
....
....
....

What do you think God is inviting you into during this season?

....
....
....
....
....
....
....
....

The Peace of Jesus

*"My peace is the legacy I leave to you. . . . Do
not let your heart be troubled or fearful."*

JOHN 14:27 THE VOICE

We could never hope to live up to the rules God laid out for the right life for us. We mess up all the time, despite our best efforts. We will never be perfect, and luckily we don't have to be because Jesus was.

When He sacrificed Himself for us, He wiped our debts clean. Paid in full.

Yet so many of us still live as if we have to earn God's love. Like if we stop striving and achieving, everything will fall apart. We are pushing from a place of fear, not faith. We know that on paper we have been saved, but we don't trust that truth with our hearts. And that is an exhausting way to live.

Jesus isn't holding anything over your head. There is no other shoe waiting to drop. No hidden contingencies. You are saved just as you are. You are loved just as you are. His peace is yours forever, and you can rest confident in that truth.

If you have accepted Jesus as your Savior, how has the concept of rest changed for you since then?

....

....

....

....

....

....

| What fears and failures do you need to let go of?

....

....

....

....

| Ask God to give you His peace and true rest.

....

....

Jesus and the Sabbath

*And He said to them, "The Son of
Man is also Lord of the Sabbath."*

LUKE 6:5 NKJV

When Jesus was growing up, the Sabbath was observed fastidiously every week. Early Christians also observed the Sabbath faithfully, choosing to come together for worship, community, and rest each week.

Over time, the concept of a Sabbath has fallen away. Many people attend church once a week, but they don't usually take the remainder of that day to rest. Instead that time is filled with kids' sports, laundry, grocery shopping, or other errands and housekeeping. And that makes sense, since time always seems to be in short supply.

However, choosing a Sabbath each week is still an option for you. It will take some planning, but you can choose to dedicate one day a week to rest and restoration for yourself and your family. That does not mean that you have to abstain from all work. Work that helps you feel recharged isn't the same as work that drains you. Spending time tending your garden or making a delicious meal with your family is technically work, but if those things are restorative for you, then they belong in your Sabbath plans.

| What would Sabbath look like for you?

....
....
....
....
....

| Which activities would you exclude?

....
....
....
....

| Which activities would you want to include every week?

....
....
....
....

Gratitude

*Return, O my soul, to your rest; for the
LORD has dealt bountifully with you.*

PSALM 116:7

Your life contains multitudes of blessings. If you've only
been focused on your problems and issues, you may find it
challenging to spot the good stuff.

You will struggle in this life. Bad things will happen. You
will lose people and things that matter to you. You will feel
lonely and sad and angry and even hopeless sometimes. You
will face situations that seem impossible. But also, God will be
there beside you through it all.

Choosing to be thankful for the good doesn't mean you are
ignoring the bad. But focusing all your energy on the tough
stuff will keep you in a constant state of stress, making it
more difficult to find rest. Instead, intentionally cultivating a
grateful heart is a healthy way to combat anxiety and lean into
rest. A grateful heart finds rest more easily and holds hope
more fully.

Acknowledging both the bad *and* the good helps keep your
perspective balanced. And spending time each day focusing on
the things you have to be grateful for helps keep you connected
to God, the Giver of all blessings, including rest.

When do you acknowledge your blessings and thank God? Is it a regular part of each day?

....
....
....
....
....
....
....
....

What are you grateful for this week?

....
....
....
....
....
....
....
....

Look and Ask

Thus says the L<small>ORD</small>: ". . . ask for the ancient paths, where the good way is; and walk in it, and find rest for your souls."

JEREMIAH 6:16

We are encouraged to pursue our passions. We're told to do what we love, but we're also counseled to find something practical to do with our lives, something that pays well or has good benefits.

Almost all the advice we receive about our careers, families, and lives assumes that we want to achieve as much as possible. We're told we can be anything, but the truth is that we can't possibly do *everything* we want at the same time. And it is exhausting trying to make sense of it all.

So how do you make everyone happy, especially yourself? You ask for God's help. Pray that He will show you the way, that He will make His path your path. Then intentionally spend time resting and abiding in Him, listening in silence, waiting for His advice. If you let Him, He will change your heart to want the same things He does for you: a life of good work, sacred rest, and profound faith.

> Describe a time when God nudged you in the right direction after you asked for His guidance.

> What did it feel or sound like? How did you know it was Him?

The Joy of Slow Living

*It is good and fitting for one to eat and
drink, and to enjoy the good of all his labor
in which he toils under the sun all the
days of his life which God gives him.*

ECCLESIASTES 5:18 NKJV

God is a Creator. He created this entire world and then made us in His own image, and He invited us to work alongside Him. Work has always been part of the story, but sometimes we get work all mixed up. So many of us fall into the trap of working to earn our identity. If work is what anchors us and identifies us in the world, we end up worshiping our work. We place work above everything else—balance and rest and joy and our health—because it defines us.

But when we choose to live in God's slow and intentional rhythm for life, we accept our identity in Christ. Then our work becomes an expression of that—a form of joy-filled worship all its own, an outpouring of that identity into the world—and it is balanced with sacred rest. We are able to work *from rest*, not rest *from work*. And that makes all the difference.

Do you rest from work or work from rest? Why is that?

....
....
....
....
....
....

What would slow living look like for you?

....
....
....
....

How could your work be seen as a form of worship?

....
....
....
....

Celebrate

*On the third day there was a wedding
at Cana in Galilee, and the mother of
Jesus was there. Jesus also was invited
to the wedding with his disciples.*

JOHN 2:1–2

We all mess up, fall down, and even fail spectacularly. But we also win sometimes. We take big, important steps. We kick bad habits. We start new relationships and deepen friendships. We graduate. We get promoted. We climb the mountain. We write the book. We create art and music. We live fiercely. And we should celebrate all of it.

Celebrations aren't rest in the traditional sense. But taking the time to acknowledge, be grateful for, and rejoice in the good gives us renewed energy and zest for life. It refuels us for the next obstacle to tackle, the next path to take, or the next season of life. Celebrations bond us more closely with those who celebrate with us, deepening our communities.

You can rush through life, always onto the next thing, eye on the uncertain future. Or you can choose to take each day as it comes, being present and rejoicing for what you have and trusting that God will give you more to celebrate tomorrow.

What are some of your favorite celebrations from your life?

....
....
....
....
....

What was the last thing you celebrated?

....
....
....
....

If you chose something to celebrate this week, what would it be, and what would you plan?

....
....
....
....

Joy

*A joyful heart is good medicine, but a
crushed spirit dries up the bones.*

PROVERBS 17:22

Countless generations have tried to wrap their very human brains around who God is. One thing we do know is that we were created in God's image. If God had been all seriousness and reverence only, we would be that way too. But we aren't.

God made us creative, hardworking, emotional, and empathetic. And He gave us a sense of humor. We make each other laugh. We find joy in small and big things, and we work hard to share that joy with others. We make up silly jokes and cheesy puns, and we tell hilarious stories to entertain one another. God filled us with His own joy and delight in things.

Joy is life-giving. Laughter and humor and silliness boost our energy levels. They chase away the negativity and cynicism that we can fall into so easily. God didn't create us to suffer through life. This week when you pray and spend time with Him, let your joyful side out and see what happens.

When was the last time you laughed so hard that you nearly cried?

....
....
....
....

Who do you enjoy spending time with the most because they make you so happy?

....
....
....
....
....

How joy-filled would you say your day-to-day life is?

....
....
....
....

Rest Gives Perspective

For his anger is but for a moment, and his favor is for a lifetime. Weeping may tarry for the night, but joy comes with the morning.

PSALM 30:5

Have you ever felt so exhausted that almost everything made you want to cry? So tired that every misstep or wrong turn felt catastrophic? Rest has a profound power to shift our perspectives. When we don't get enough rest, everything seems more difficult, more frustrating, and more discouraging. When we do get plenty of rest, even the biggest obstacles seem smaller, there is more joy to be found, and our hearts are more grateful. Life feels easier when we are operating at full capacity, and to get to full capacity, we have to rest and take care of ourselves.

A lot of problems that feel big in the moment are much smaller than they seem and can be solved with a little self-care, such as a nourishing meal and a hot shower. These things may not solve your problems, but they will make you feel better, and you will be better equipped to actually solve your problems after a little replenishment.

What types of self-care do you practice when you feel stuck on a problem or find yourself having big feelings about something?

....
....
....
....

When have you found an issue easier to deal with after some self-care?

....
....
....
....

What other, bigger issues are you dealing with that may be easier to tackle with more rest?

....
....
....
....

Find Rest in Community

*Day by day, attending the temple together and
breaking bread in their homes, they received
their food with glad and generous hearts.*

ACTS 2:46

It seems that people are lonelier than ever before, and it's taking a toll. Many people experience social isolation—in other words, they don't have a close confidant or meaningful relationships, or they just feel alone most of the time. Are you one of them?

Some studies suggest that loneliness is dangerous for your mental and physical health, similar to smoking. Staying isolated is killing us.

The kind of deep, intimate relationships we can find rest and acceptance in don't just happen. We have to be intentional about cultivating them. Community isn't found; it's made. Choice by choice. Word by word. Action by action.

When we choose community, we are choosing to live like Jesus. We are choosing to embrace the messiness of loving those who are different from us, sometimes in every possible way. And that is life-giving.

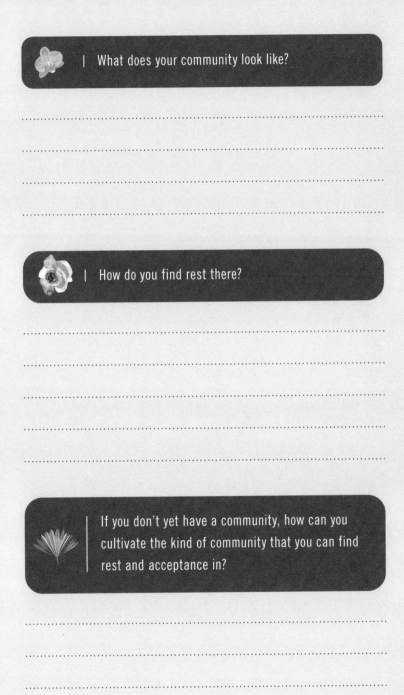

| What does your community look like?

....
....
....
....

| How do you find rest there?

....
....
....
....
....

If you don't yet have a community, how can you cultivate the kind of community that you can find rest and acceptance in?

....
....
....
....

Embrace Nature

*The L*ORD *. . . makes me lie down in green pastures. He leads me beside still waters.*

PSALM 23:1–2

God created this beautiful world out of nothing. Everything from the smallest bacteria to the largest tree came from His imagination, all designed to follow the cycles of life and growth, death and rebirth that He set in motion. It's hard to grasp just how amazing that truly is, but our world is a living miracle.

Regular time spent in nature feeds our souls. When our human-created expectations, technology, and culture have worn you out, and you desperately need rest, it's time to develop a nature habit. Sit on the grass, breathe the fresh air, and let the sun warm your face. Walk through a park or forest or along a shoreline, and truly observe everything around you. Breathe in the scent of freshly turned earth or wildflowers or growing herbs. Feel the softness of spring leaves or the chill of snowflakes on your skin.

Find rest in God's creation. Let nature remind you how big and bold and wild God is too.

| How often do you get outside?

....
....
....
....
....

| What outdoor hobby could you commit to regularly?

....
....
....
....
....

Have you ever been somewhere in nature that made you feel how big God is?

....
....
....
....

Flourish

The fruit of the Spirit is love, joy,
peace, patience, kindness, goodness,
faithfulness, gentleness, self-control;
against such things there is no law.

GALATIANS 5:22–23

Being busy or accomplishing a lot is not the same as bearing fruit. Staying busy may make us feel like we are making progress, but it actually keeps us stunted and stuck. Busyness crowds out the things we need to actually grow and bear fruit. Things like rest, connection, joy, and faith.

Getting through work or earning accolades is about *doing* something. Bearing fruit is about *becoming* someone—someone more like Jesus. We do that by developing a close relationship with Him.

When we live our lives intimately with Jesus, choosing Him again and again, He changes us from the inside out. We grow and blossom and flourish, and we become the people we were always meant to be. People who are loving, joyful, peace-filled, patient, kind, good, faithful, gentle, generous, and thoughtful. These things are the outpouring of a life deeply rooted in the soil of truth, watered with grace, and nourished by hope. When we choose to be faithful, God makes us fruitful.

How much of your busyness is optional? How much is a necessity?

Which optional things can you eliminate so you can spend more time with Jesus?

What fruit is your life bearing right now?

Find Joy in Nourishment and Rest

*I know there is nothing better for us than
to be joyful and to do good throughout our
lives; to eat and drink and see the good in
all of our hard work is a gift from God.*

ECCLESIASTES 3:12–13 The Voice

We all know that we need to get more rest and take better care of ourselves. Sometimes we feel guilty when we don't do these things because they feel like chores. But living a more rest-filled life isn't a chore at all. It's a gift. And we get to choose whether or not to accept it.

God isn't going to force us into His rhythm. Just like He doesn't force us to accept Jesus or force us to have a relationship with Him. But He does promise us that living life with Him is a joy, not a burden.

A life lived God's way is balance and rhythm, repeating cycles and seasons. It's the joy found in true, sacred rest and a secure knowledge of our identity and purpose. It's putting down deep roots in fertile soil and growing over time. It's community and work and worship and joy and peace and always God to lean on.

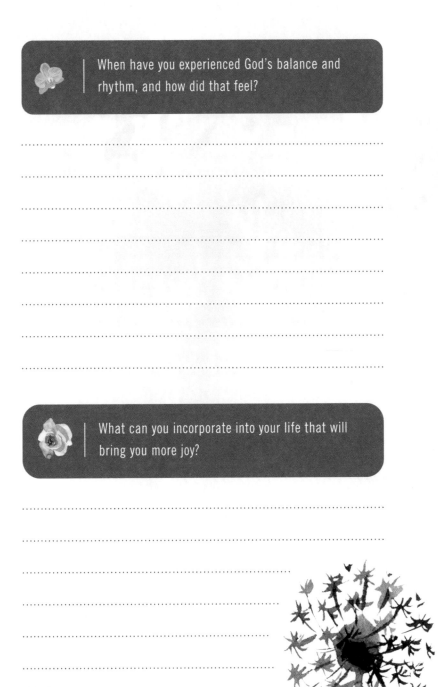

When have you experienced God's balance and rhythm, and how did that feel?

....

....

....

....

....

....

....

What can you incorporate into your life that will bring you more joy?

....

....

....

....

....

....

....

....

CHANGE HOW YOU LOOK AT YOUR LIFE

ISBN: 978-0-310-46172-2

THE WEEKLY PURPOSE PROJECT

What lights a fire in your heart? What are you uniquely suited to do? How do you take the talents God gave you to the next level? *The Weekly Purpose Project* is a 52-week guided journal that offers a transformational journey to guide you through discovering how to create a life of purpose and chase your dreams.

CELEBRATE PROGRESS OVER PERFECTION

ISBN: 978-0-310-46410-5

THE WEEKLY HABITS PROJECT

This beautiful yearlong guided journal will help you build life-giving habits, set achievable goals, and enjoy spiritual growth with each grace-filled step forward.